BAXTER
and the
Trolls that lost

PRISCILLA

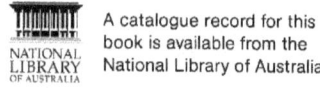 A catalogue record for this book is available from the National Library of Australia

Copyright © 2024 Sue Rushton

All rights are reserved. No part of this book may be reproduced in any way or form without the permission of the author.

This book is a work of fiction. The characters and situations are a product of the writer's imagination and are not to be constructed as real.

ISBN-13: 978-1-923174-30-6

Linellen Press
265 Boomerang Road
Oldbury, Western Australia
www.linellenpress.com.au

Dedication

To all the beautiful children.

May your light of kindness

shine brighter than the stars

of a midnight desert plain.

Acknowledgement

I have been extremely lucky to have worked with the highly successful artist David Giles. Thank you, David, for your generosity. I am humbled by your kindness.

Poem

Into my thoughts you creep

your disdainful words wrap around me

like a web of deceit

where pity and pain align to undermine

and cut me so deep.

Your venomous swirl of words

leap out to greet and defeat,

holding your desire to reap the cause

of some poor soul's permanent sleep.

"**Be Not** that, my friend".

Contents

Dedication 3

Poem 5

Contents 7

True buddy 8

Trolls 17

Home amongst the trees 25

Beach holidays 31

Heart of me 35

True buddy

That's me down the hill, in the back seat, the wind blowing my ears around in and out of the car window as we roll into the art house where David – Davo – Daddio – or "DADDAH" works.

He's my human. He teaches art classes, a cool dude – people dig his vibe. He is kind to everyone ... yeah, that's my Daddah.

He saved me from a life of hell and starvation. Being on the streets was scary. No one wanted me. By the time he found me, I looked pretty scroungy with wiry, stinky, black-brown hair, a big scrawny body and piercing brown eyes like a Kelpie. But he took me in and saved me.

Since then, we have shared everything. We are best buddies and go everywhere together.

Daddah stands up at the front of the class. I like messing around and having fun. I sit up with one paw up on the rocks, like an overseer wearing a masterful look on my face, keeping that grungy lot in order.

One by one, as students arrive, I run to greet them, racing down the wooden hallway, putting on the brakes, getting into a slide just before they enter the doorway.

Sometimes I crash right into them, accidentally on purpose. The students laugh and greet me.

'Baxter, how are you doing?'

'Baxter, you're boisterous today!'

They know I'm the special one, really, I'm the boss of everything.

Once things get going most of the crew give me a pat as I walk around them. I give each one a few sniffs around the ankles, sometimes up the leg if they smell doggy – not the ones that smell a bit rank. I have my favorites though.

Daddah is kind. He takes in everyone, the cray-cray ones, the crusty old ones, the young ones, anyone really. Daddah once told me, 'The best are the ones who need the most help.'

He said, 'Those dudes are a gift to us all because we learn how lucky we are to share and show kindness.'

When class is going on, I do the rounds to check out the lunch bags sniffing around them. Sometimes the wafting smell of bacon sandwiches draws me in for a closer look.

One day, Betty shooed me away from her bag. To be honest, I never really liked her. She screeches her words out like a whining cat. I have very sensitive ears and cringe every time she talks.

Casually, I sauntered back onto the lawn for a while, eyeballing her as the sun beat down, warming my coat.

Sometimes, I like to play a trick or two, like sidling up to one of my fans for a pat and then, when they bend closer, I bark right in their faces.

It cracks me up when they lurch backward in surprise. I love to entertain them. It works every time. Otherwise, I wait until they have all settled and are engrossed in their art work then run bounding down the passage, through the glass door, around the corner and jump onto the platform where they are all working.

It causes such a stir. Laughter abounds at my antics. It's the best fun.

Trolls

One day after class, when all the students had left, I heard a wailing sound from inside and panicked. It sounded like Daddah.

I raced down the passage, sliding around the corner.

There he was, curled up limp on the floor, gasping, his body heaving with smothered cries like a whimpering baby.

I ran to his side, licked his face all over and over until he lifted his arm and put it around my neck. He cried some more into my neck. Tears rolled down his face onto my coat, which ended up dripping wet.

His deep breaths slowly subsided. Daddah said; 'Baxter, 'I feel like I can't breathe. I'm so hurt by what the online trolls, strangers be them, posted about my artwork over the internet: stuff like 'That's not art, it's rubbish, crap! A baby could do better than that!'

'Why? Why were those vultures poking shit at me for everyone to see? They are like thieves stealing my self-worth.

'I feel like a fake, like hiding from the world. I'm wounded, shamed and embarrassed.'

Daddah's mood was dark. He said to me, 'To make it worse, my own head voices are poking shit at me as well now, telling me ... 'You should vanish, just die' over and over again, like a wheel spinning round and round.

Daddah said, 'Baxter, I tried to figure it out but I don't understand how people can be so mean and horrible.'

He rehashed what they said – it had crushed him like a giant tree branch smacking him in the face.

The faceless vultures tap away, pick, pick, picking at you with their venomous sprays, hiding away from the world anonymously. They just want to get off on being mean to bring people down.

What's wrong with them? They're not normal, just brainless fools!

I felt sad for Daddah. He is the best. So caring, especially to those who no one else gives a crap about ... people and animals alike.

I decided to play a game, tugging at his sleeve. Then I ran, picked up his phone in my mouth, took it, and dropped it in his lap.

Daddah decided to call his friend Vivien. He tearfully shared his thoughts and feelings. Daddah seemed better after that. Then he talked to me about it, like redirecting negative vibes, not allowing them to manifest in his head.

Daddah sat in silence, so I tuned into his vibe and our energy merged.

He focused on his own heart, love, energy and gratitude. I knew this was the greatest power of all. That's how I got through hard times.

Daddah put more time into his stillness; he changed and became more settled.

I'm so proud of Daddah. He turned ugly negative thoughts into peacefulness. He turned a bad situation into better energy, then put it out there in his mind for the love to be shared and multiplied a million times back into the universe.

Home amongst the trees

I drove Daddah home that day and he sat curled up in the back seat of the car. I was still annoyed at the nasty dudes wrecking his day. I felt like doing a rotten fart and sending it to them in a bottle, but I know that's the wrong way to go about things.

Nasty-smelly attracts nasty-smelly so I gave that idea a miss.

When we got home, Daddah made a tasty stew. Ooohh, I loved it – fresh gravy beef and veggies.

We snuggled up in the lounge together and watched a movie. Daddah was still a bit sniffly but in a much better space.

He said to me, 'Baxter, just because people put shit on you it doesn't mean you have to eat it.'

'Now I just think back to the sender. You go. Release it from my mind and then spend time in my heart space, the fixer in life.'

I felt so proud of Daddah.

It was a peaceful day and my mind drifted off, thinking about the special sausages Daddah buys 'just for me'.

Mmmm, I can't wait to get home and hang around the kitchen. He usually cranks up the music, generally Led Zeppelin.

I prefer Van Morrison myself, more Zen for my ears. Anyway, we're together, so it's no big deal; it doesn't matter.

Daddah called me over. 'Baxter, here's a piece of cheese.'

Mmmm, my favorite snack. I stumbled a bit and lost my balance and nearly smacked my head on the ground, but Daddah caught me just in time. Then he got me checked over by the vet.

A few tests resulted in nothing out of the normal so I got the all-clear.

The sun was shining and life went on in the usual way. Daddah was doing his thing, painting, talking to the class. Just his presence makes everyone happy and free with laughter. I felt like the luckiest dog alive. It couldn't get any better for a mut like me, surrounded by kind loving humans.

Beach holidays

The traffic was heavy. We had many stops to do on the way home. We were getting ready to go on our favourite holiday down south. I love walking along the sandy beach with Daddah, checking out all the other dogs and smells amongst the trees.

Ooh-wah! A stabbing pain raced through my head, and all of a sudden, I felt sick, weird, disoriented.

I felt a warm dribble slide down from my nose. I put my tongue out to catch it – yuck, it tasted like blood.

I felt weak, so quietly I wandered off to a shady spot to rest and recover.

After a while, the pain in my head went away. Daddah was snoozing on his beach chair. He hadn't noticed me being any different so I got up and pretended nothing was wrong.

We always spend a few weeks this time of year just relaxing, Daddah and me. Sometimes, we go mooching around or fishing. I love scratching around in the sand on the beach while Daddah tries to catch a fish.

When he's got one on the line, I bounce over, trying to grab the fish while he's pulling it in. It causes a big ruckus, Daddah yelling, 'Baxter! Baxter, stop!' as he strides backward, laughing.

Heart of me

When we got back from holidays, life went on in its usual way: driving up and down from the hills to art classes and then back again. We shared our special times together at night, eating dinner, cuddling up on the lounge, watching TV, and sometimes listening to his music. Life is good, really good. Daddah and I make a great team.

Lots of friends gathered next to the waterfall garden. Daddah was there standing next to my favorite garden bed. It has a stunning display of flowers with good sniffability.

Lots of the art dudes and some of his family were there. Daddah had a funny jar and my special treats in his hand. I wondered what he was doing with them.

He said some funny things about my antics that made people laugh and some nice things at my ... funeral?

Tears rolled down Daddah's face. He let out a screeching cry that came from deep down inside his guts, churning out like the sound of a pup howling for his mummy.

I was touched by his words, his sensitivity and love for me (the scrawny, stinky one; me, Baxter, the homeless dog who got lucky).

People who attended my funeral put flowers on my grave in that nice garden.

Daddah spread my ashes while he talked about how much fun we shared. Daddah's face was still scrunched up, his head hung down in sorrow, tears dripping from behind his sunglasses.

I looked down on him with love and gratitude – this life was done.

Daddah swiped at his neck and groaned. 'Ugh, my neck is slobbery wet … damn sticky weather.'

I chuckled to myself. I can still play tricks from above and laid another lick on his neck. What fun I will have annoying him. I'm now just pure love from above, like a love bubble that never bursts.

Daddah gingerly made his way home.

After, he and his friend Vivien were going far away to travel to different places. Daddah had always wanted to travel but he wanted to do it without me. Well, at least that's what he thinks.

About the Author

Priscilla has worked for many years in her field with attained qualifications in Sociology and Psychology (BA) as well as qualifications in Counseling (Dip). She also practices alternative therapies and has an interest in the arts. She has a love of the environment and animals, the outback red dirt places, the beach and hot summer days. Priscilla lives in Perth, Western Australia. Her biggest love and most valued role has been as a mother to her sons, who have been her greatest teachers in life.

www.ingramcontent.com/pod-product-compliance
Lightning Source LLC
Chambersburg PA
CBHW041153110526
44590CB00027B/4220